David Livingstone

his life and work as told through the media of postage stamps and allied material

Peter J. Westwood

All royalties from the sales of this title are donated to
the David Livingstone Trust, Blantyre, Glasgow,
Scotland.

Published for
Jamieson & Munro
by
Holmes McDougall Ltd., Edinburgh.

Published for Jamieson & Munro by Holmes McDougall Ltd.,
Allander House, 137-141 Leith Walk, Edinburgh EH6 8NS.

Typesetting and printing by Sunprint, 40 Craigs, Stirling and 36 Tay Street,
Perth, Scotland.

Printed on Success Satin made in Scotland for Wiggins Teape Paper,
Livingston, at Donside Paper Mills, Aberdeen.

Design and artwork, Arthur Ingham, "Perthshire Advertiser".

British Library cataloguing in publication data.

Westwood, Peter J.
  David Livingstone: his life and work.
  1. Livingstone, David, *1813-1873*
  2. Explorers — Scotland — Biography
  3. Explorers — Africa — Biography
  I. Title
  916.7'04   DT731.L8

ISBN 0-7157-2599-5

CONTENTS

Page

Foreword 5

Introduction 7

Blantyre — London 1813-1840 9

Africa 1841-1843 15

Missionary Years 1849-1854 18

Across Africa 1854-1856 22

Victoria Falls 1855 25

Welcome Home 1856-1858 29

Return to Africa 1858-1860 31

Lake Nyasa 1861-1863 35

Shupanga 37

Fund Raising 1864-1865 39

Lake Mweru and Bangweulu 1866-1871 41

Henry Morton Stanley 1871-1872 43

Last Journey 1872-1873 47

ACKNOWLEDGMENTS

Grateful acknowledgments are made to the following:—

The Church of Scotland Overseas Council for permission to use illustrations from their folder 'Livingstone and After'. The Postal Authorities of countries whose stamps are reproduced throughout the book. Bob Matthews, Motherwell for the photograph on page 6. The Clydesdale Bank P.L.C. Stanley Hunter, Glasgow, the editor of the Scottish Stamp Catalogue and ALBA Stamp Club Journal. William Cunningham, Warden the David Livingstone National Memorial, Blantyre. The late Jean Clark, Paisley. Margaret McIntyre, Newton Mearns. Alex McInnes, Kilbarchan. Ken Norris, Hamilton. Charles McBain, "Hamilton Advertiser". Arthur Ingham, "Perthshire Advertiser". Jenkins & Jardine, Solicitors & Notaries, (J. J. Munro Trust), Stirling.

Burn Bank Road
Hamilton 24 May
1865

My Dear Friend
Shall be
very much pleased
to see you at any
time you can
call — Though my
time is usually
very much
occupied
Yours ever affy

David Livingstone

Rev'd John Kirk
27 Greenhill Gardens
Edinburgh

D L

A letter and envelope written by Dr. Livingstone to the Rev. John Kirk during his last visit to his homeland.
It was common practice for the explorer to initial the front of envelopes 'Dr. L.' or 'D.L.'.

FOREWORD

David Livingstone set sail for Africa at the end of 1840, the year significant to philatelists for the introduction of penny postage by Sir Rowland Hill. Both men were to be honoured in Westminster Abbey.

Livingstone's life, from Blantyre, Scotland, through years of missionary endeavour, travel and exploration in southern and central Africa to his death near Lake Bangweulu, has been often told. It has been fascinatingly illustrated by Peter Westwood with his knowledge of the postage stamps from thirty years of centenary commemorations.

When Rhodesia and Nyasaland issued the first postage stamp to portray my great-grandfather I was working in what became Zambia and have visited Blantyre — Malawi — Livingstonia and the Victoria Falls — Mosioatunya. It, therefore, gives me particular pleasure to introduce this book to its readers.

Over ten years have passed since David Livingstone featured on African and British stamps but in under thirty years the bicentenary of his birth will come. I believe this will not be overlooked in African countries where to this day he is remembered and respected.

David L. Wilson.

The house at Blantyre, Scotland where Dr Livingstone was born in 1813. Photograph circa 1900.

APART from Dr Livingstone's own accounts of his travels many other books have been written about his life and works. This book does not try to emulate any of what has been written before, and it adds no new found knowledge to the life of this great Scotsman. The purpose of this book is to give a brief chronological account of the life of Dr Livingstone through the media of the postage stamp and allied material.

The first time Dr Livingstone's portrait appeared on a postage stamp was in 1955 on an issue from Rhodesia and Nyasaland to mark the centenary of his discovery of the Victoria Falls.

Robert Burns was the first Scot to appear on a British postage stamp in 1966. However, it was appropriate that Dr Livingstone should be honoured by the British Post Office in 1973 with a single value stamp. This issue co-incided with the anniversary of his death a hundred years earlier. His friend and fellow explorer Henry Stanley also appeared on a stamp issued at the same time. Earlier in 1968 his portrait did appear philatelically, on the outside cover of a Post Office booklet of stamps — the first Scot accorded this honour. In order to tell this story I have included a number of stamps, postmarks and illustrations which have only a loose connection with Dr Livingstone. For example the illustration on page 19 shows the capital of Angola — St. Paul do Loanda. Dr Livingstone visited Loanda on 31st May, 1854 during his Trans-Africa Expedition of 1853-1856.

Above and right: Stamps issued by Rhodesia and Nyasaland in 1955 to mark the Centenary of the discovery of the Victoria Falls by Dr Livingstone.

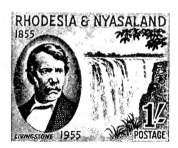

Right: Dr Livingstone featured on the cover of a British Post Office booklet of stamps issued in 1968.

Below: Stamp from Malawi featuring the new Post Office Sorting Office in Blantyre and stamp issued by Nyasaland in 1953 on the subject of Grading Cotton.

DAVID LIVINGSTONE was born in a house in Shuttle Row, Blantyre, eight miles south of Glasgow in Scotland, on 19th March, 1813. His ancestors in the name of his grandfather having come from Ulva in the Hebrides. One great grandfather fought and died at the Battle of Culloden.

At the time of writing, Blantyre in Scotland has not been illustrated on a postage stamp. However, mail posted at the National Memorial to Dr. Livingstone in Blantyre can have a special cachet applied (on application to the warden) which illustrates the explorers birthplace.

The word "Blantyre" has appeared on many types of postal cancellations dating back to pre-stamp times until the present day use by the Post Office at Blantyre. Blantyre in Malawi (formerly Nyasaland) received its name from a Church of Scotland Mission in 1876, after the birthplace of David Livingstone and like Blantyre in Scotland has yet to feature directly on a postage stamp although a number of buildings, roads and installations in Blantyre, Malawi have been featured on stamps. The word Blantyre also appears on an assortment of postal cancellations. To mark the centenary of the founding of the Mission at Blantyre, the Malawi Postal Authority overprinted two of their definitive stamps in 1976 for the occasion with words "Blantyre Mission Centenary 1876-1976".

David Livingstone commenced work in the cotton mills at Blantyre at the age of ten, working from six in the morning until eight at night with a half hour break for

Top left: Battle of Culloden anniversary postmark and left: special cachet applied to mail from the National Memorial at Blantyre.

breakfast and an hour for lunch — six days a week.

His first job was that of a "piecer" which meant that he had to piece together threads on the spinning frames when they looked like breaking. He was still working in the mill at the age of 21 but by then was a spinner.

It was David Livingstone's Zambesi Expedition of 1858 that first introduced cotton gins into what is now called Malawi. It could therefore be said that he was instrumental in starting what was to become one of Malawi's top agricultural industries — Cotton. This important industry was featured on stamps from Nyasaland in 1953 and 1954, by Malawi in 1964 and Uganda in 1975.

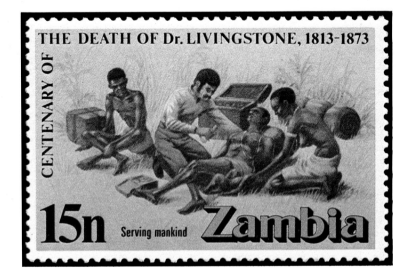

Above and right: Stamps from Southern Rhodesia and Zambia featuring Dr Livingstone as a Medical Man.

MEDICAL MAN

In the autumn of 1836 David Livingstone entered Anderson's College, a Glasgow medical school and found lodgings in a street called Rotten Row — the price of the room being two shillings a week. At this time he also studied theology at a congregational seminary and during this period he met James Young of Kelly, a chemist who invented a process for distilling oil from shale, he was nicknamed "Sir Paraffin" by Livingstone. James Young became a life-long friend and correspondent and helped to finance Livingstone's last expedition.

In 1840 David Livingstone received the Diploma of the Faculty of Physicians and Surgeons from the Andersonian College in George Street, Glasgow.

The first stamp issued and believed to be showing Livingstone as a medical man was released in Southern Rhodesia in 1953. Stanley Gibbons stamp catalogue illustrates this stamp with the caption "Medical Services" while the Rhodesia catalogue carries the caption "Medical aid by Dr Livingstone and modern Rhodesia". To mark the centenary of his death, Zambia (formerly Northern Rhodesia) issued a set of stamps one of which shows the Doctor attending Africans in the bush with the caption "Serving Mankind".

MISSIONARY

On 5th September, 1838 Livingstone was accepted as a Missionary by the London Missionary Society, and after passing the test examination he was sent for training to a small Missionary College at Chipping Ongar, Essex, England. During 1973 a Livingstone Centenary Exhibition was held at Ongar and the British Post Office issued a special cancellation for the occasion showing a map of Africa and a broken slave chain. Also that year the London Missionary Society franked their outgoing mail with a special meter cancellation which included the portrait of Dr Livingstone.

On his return to London from Ongar he was accommodated in a boarding house for young Missionaries in Aldersgate and on 20th November, 1840 was ordained a Missionary at Albion Chapel, Finsbury, London.

Livingstone holding a bible and reading to a group of Africans is shown on a stamp from Zambia in 1973 with an appropriate title "Blessed are they" and also that year Malawi issued a stamp and a souvenir sheet showing the stained glass window of the Livingstonia Mission in Northern Malawi in which the Doctor is seen with local chiefs against a background of Lake Malawi. During his stay in London, Livingstone met Dr Robert Moffat for the first time, and Moffat's account of his Mission work in Africa challenged Livingstone's imagination, and on enquiring from Moffat if he would

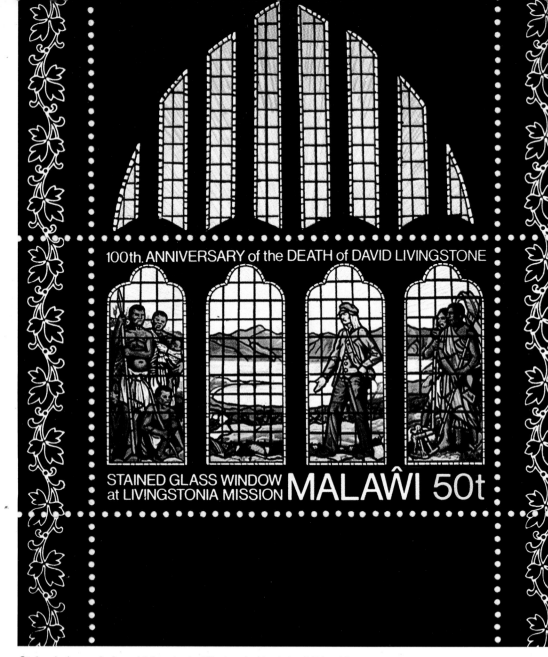

Stained glass window, Livingstonia Mission in Northern Malawi featured on a souvenir sheet to mark the 100th Anniversary of the death of Dr Livingstone.

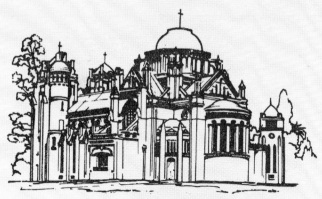

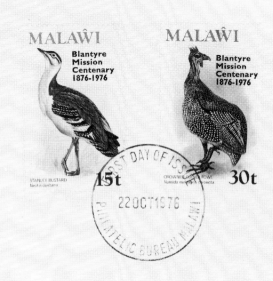

Commemorative cover with the two Malawi definitive stamps overprinted to mark the Centenary of the founding of the Mission at Blantyre.

do for Africa, Moffat Said, "Yes, if you are prepared to leave occupied land and push to the North". Not so many years later he was to meet Moffat again in Africa and eventually marry his daughter, Mary, who was born in Africa at Kuruman on 12th April, 1821.

In 1972 Rhodesia issued a commemorative stamp in their "Famous Figure" series showing Dr Robert Moffat who like Livingstone was also born in Scotland. Moffat set up a Mission at Inyati, near the King's Kraal in 1859 which became the first white settlement in what was later to become Rhodesia.

On 8th December, 1840, Livingstone aged 27 sailed from London in the "George" bound for South Africa to commence work as a Missionary and from this starting point he was to become one of the world's greatest explorers.

Top right: Ongar postmark with broken slave chain.
Top left: Dr Livingstone preaching to natives on a stamp from Zambia.
Right: Cover from Rhodesia commemorating Dr Robert Moffat.

Above: Capetown.
Circa 1840s.

Left: Dr Robert Moffat,
Livingstone's father-in-law.

Right: Cancellation used at
Moffat Mission, Kuruman.

1841
1843
AFRICA

LIVINGSTONE'S journey to Africa in the "George" was not without trouble, during a gale one of the masts split, forcing the captain to make a detour to Rio de Janeiro for repairs. The voyage took three months, eventually anchoring in Simon's Bay on 14th March, 1841. A few days later Dr Livingstone was in Capetown in what was then the Cape of Good Hope.

Although the first adhesive postage stamps in the world were issued in Great Britain in 1840 — the now famous Penny Black and Twopenny Blue — there were no postage stamps as such when Livingstone arrived in Africa in 1841. The first postage stamp in that part of the African Continent did not appear until 1853 in the form of the Cape of Good Hope triangular stamp. Both the Penny Black, Twopenny Blue and the Cape triangular stamps are now collectors items under the "classic" heading.

On 16th April, Dr Livingstone once more boarded the "George" this time bound for Algoa Bay, some 450 miles to the east of the Cape on his way to Kuruman, a remote Mission Station roughly 600 miles inland and north of Algoa Bay. The Doctor arrived at Kuruman in Bechuanaland (or Botswana) as it is now called, on 31st July, 1841. He was to stay in Kuruman for two years and after having many disappointments about his role there as a Missionary he was ready to embark on his own missionary work. This came about in June, 1843 when he received permission from the London Missionary Society to establish a Mission to the north of Kuruman. In the August of that year he set out to reconnoitre a site

The first adhesive postage stamp in the world.

for a Mission at Mabotsa, 250 miles north of Kuruman. Dr Livingstone's first meeting in Africa with Dr Robert Moffat was on the Moffat's return to Kuruman on 13th December, 1843, and was also his first meeting with Moffat's two daughters Ann and Mary. He must have got to know Mary quite well during his two weeks stay at Kuruman, for he decided on his next visit to the Moffats he would formally ask for her hand in marriage.

AFTER leaving Kuruman, Dr Livingstone was on his way back to Mabotsa when he was to have a frightening experience with a lion. Two years earlier he had seen a woman devoured in her garden by a lion, the area around Mabotsa appeared to have more than its fair share of these noble beasts.

On 16th February, 1844, some natives asked Dr Livingstone to help them kill a lion that had just dragged off some of their sheep, he agreed, but after firing both barrels at the lion he only succeeded in wounding it. While trying to re-load his gun the lion jumped catching him by the arm, shook him "as a terrier dog does a rat" causing his upper arm to splinter leaving him with a permanent shortened left arm.

Mabalwe, a native teacher whom he had brought from Kuruman, seeing that his master might be killed by the lion snatched a gun from another native and aimed both barrels at the lion. The gun misfired causing the lion to leave Dr Livingstone and attack his new assailant,

fortunately for all, the lion suddenly dropped dead, presumably from the gunshot wounds earlier inflicted. The African lion has been featured on many stamps, however, a single value issued in Bechuanaland in 1961 is most appropriate on this occasion for the attack took place in that country.

Dr Livingstone was very ill after this attack, nevertheless he made an astounding recovery and within three months was able to commence work on building his own house. During July of 1844 he left Mabotsa for a period of convalescence and stayed with the Moffats for three weeks, during which time he proposed to Mary and was accepted. The marriage took place on 9th January, 1845 and the couple went to live in the Mission house at Mabotsa which had been built by Livingstone.

During 1845 the Livingstone's moved from Mabotsa forty miles north to found Chonuane Mission, and they moved again the following year to establish a Mission at Kolobeng.

Top left: Moffat Institution, Kuruman.

Left: Stamp from Bechuanaland featuring an African Lion.

Attack by a lion in Bechuanaland in 1844.

1849
1854

MISSIONARY YEARS

Discovery of Lake Ngami by Livingstone, Oswell and Murray.

MISSIONARY YEARS

ON 1st June, 1849, Dr Livingstone and his family* together with two Englishmen, Oswell and Murray left the Mission to explore the interior and he was to have many disappointing and exciting experiences before arriving at Loanda, the capital of Angola on 31st May, 1854.

Loanda features on a number of map stamps issued while under the authority of the Portuguese.

Livingstone and his party were to meet many different tribes during these journeys and two which come to mind, the Barotse and Quisamas are both featured on postage stamps. The first from Zambia in 1964 to commemorate Independence showing a Barotse dancer and the latter on a stamp from Angola in 1957 showing a Quisamas woman.

Another tribe the Makololo which was particularly faithful to Dr Livingstone could be said to feature on a postage stamp issued by British Central Africa in 1891.

* During this journey Livingstone returned to the Cape with his family where he sent them home to England, he stated "I at once resolved to save my family from exposure in this unhealthy region by sending them to England, and to return alone, with a view to exploring the country in search of a healthy district that might prove a centre of civilisation and open up the interior by a path to the east or west coast".

Above: the Tse-tse fly illustrated in Livingstone's book "Missionary Travels and Researches in South Africa".
Right: Barotse Dancer featured on a stamp from Zambia.

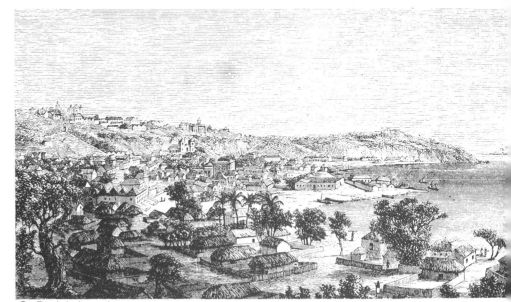

St. Paul de Loanda.

British Central Africa stamp issued in 1891 featuring the Makololo tribe.

The two natives on the stamp, one holding a spade, the other a pick represent mining and coffee growing and are also meant to represent the Makololo tribe, and although there is no proof some people like to think that the two represent Susi and Chuma, Livingstone's most faithful servants.

The dreaded Kalahari desert was crossed and the whole party suffered from drought on many occasions and probably what was just as distressing was the number of attacks they suffered from mosquitos, especially Dr Livingstone's young children, and if that was not enough, the tse-tse fly threatened to destroy their cattle which at that time were their sole means of transport. Dr Livingstone lost around forty-three cattle during this voyage.

Both these insects have appeared many times on postage stamps. As the party were travelling through Angola the stamp issued in 1962 by the Angolan Post Office to publicise Malaria Eradication fits the bill.

The party were to make many discoveries such as Lake Ngami on 1st August, 1849, and the Upper Zambesi in the centre of the continent on 4th August, 1851. Dr Livingstone in his book "Missionary Travels and Researches in South Africa" states "The discovery of the Zambesi was a most important point, for that river was not previously known to exist there at all. The Portuguese maps all represent it as rising far to the east of where we now were". Lake Ngami can be seen on a map stamp from Botswana issued in 1975 while a

Below: Botswana map stamp showing Lake Ngami.

Below: Angolan stamp featuring a Quisamas Dancer.

Above: Postmark featuring an Elephant and Muzungula (sausage) tree.

Top left: Stamp from Botswana showing fishing on the Chobe River.

Left: Flying-Boat taking off from the Zambesi River.

Rhodesia and Nyasaland stamp issued in 1962 shows a flying-boat taking off from the Zambesi. Mozambique also issued a stamp showing a bridge over the Zambesi and a number of map stamps also include the river.

Another river, the Chobe, also very familiar to Dr Livingstone and his party was the subject of a stamp issued in 1967 by Botswana to publicise the Chobe Game Reserve and shows a Chobe Bush-Buck and fishing on the river. The special commemorative postmark used by the Botswana Post Office in connection with this issue of stamps features an elephant and Muzungula (sausage) tree. This tree was Dr Livingstone's landmark and the place where he first sighted the Zambesi river, he also preached there on the morning of November 16, 1855. Dr Livingstone and his new African Makololo party; the others had stayed behind either at Kuruman or the Cape during Dr Livingstone's return of his family to the Cape arrived at Loanda on 31st May, 1854 with Livingstone a "mere bag of bones" owing mainly to his many attacks of malaria.

ACROSS AFRICA

1854 1856

The fish Pseudotropheus Livingstonii.

Left: An Eland featured on a stamp from Angola.

Below: African Buffalos and Hippopotamus featured on stamps from Malawi and Rhodesia.

A few months after arriving at Loanda, Dr Livingstone set off again, this time to cross Africa from East to West and as with the journey to Loanda many exciting discoveries were to be made.

The most famous being his discovery of the Victoria Falls on 16th November, 1855. Owing to the importance of this discovery I have devoted a separate chapter to the "Falls". From a philatelic point of view it is most important owing to the number of stamps which illustrate this world famous beauty spot.

Dr Livingstone faced many dangers not only from the hostile natives, but from the many wild animals which abound in the Zambesi basin. On one occasion Dr Livingstone narrowly escaped death from a malicious attack by a buffalo and on another occasion while travelling down the Zambesi a female hippopotamus overturned their boat leaving everyone to swim for the shore. An African buffalo appears on a stamp from Malawi issued in 1981, while the hippo can be seen on a South African definitive stamp of 1954 and on a Rhodesian stamp in 1970.

On the subject of wild life Angola issued a stamp in 1953

Above: Stamp from Malawi featuring Livingstone's Loerie.

Above and below left: Stamps from Malawi featuring the Antelope Livingstone's Suni.

featuring an Eland, *Taurotragus Oryx Livingstonii*. While Malawi issued a definitive stamp in 1971 and a commemorative stamp in 1981 featuring Livingstone's Suni which is the smallest of the many Malawi antelopes. Earlier, in 1968 Malawi issued a high value definitive stamp which featured the bird, Livingstone's Loerie and the fish *Pseudotropheus Livingstonii* has also appeared on a stamp from Malawi. The bird Livingstone's Loerie was named after Livingstone's brother Charles.

THE VICTORIA FALLS

MANY people believe that the discovery of the Victoria Falls by Dr Livingstone was probably the highlight of his many exciting discoveries, from a philatelic angle this certainly is the case.

On 16th November, 1855, Dr Livingstone had his first sight of the grandeur of the Victoria Falls as the waters of the Zambesi tore headlong over the 1600 metres wide ledge, down into the chasm over 1000 metres below. This was the first of the very few occasions that he put any other name than that of African on his map, he named the Falls "Victoria" after Queen Victoria. He justifies himself for doing this since the Falls earlier still, known as "Shongwe" had been renamed "Mosi-oa-tunya" by the Makololo—said Livingstone "If they can change the name, so can I".

Dr Livingstone had two earlier opportunities to visit the Falls in 1851 and 1853 when he was only four days distant, but apparently preferred to do missionary work rather than exploration.

The Victoria Falls was established as a settlement in November, 1898, and was originally situated on the north bank of the Zambesi River, about three miles above the actual Falls. The old site was renamed Livingstone and a definitive stamp issued in Zambia in 1968 shows the National Museum at Livingstone, there are also a number of "Livingstone" postal cancellations.

The first time the words "Victoria Falls" appeared on a postmark was in 1901. This postmark is most interesting and is now a collectors item and very rare indeed it bears the following wording "Victoria Falls, S. Africa". A Zambian stamp of 1973 shows Dr Livingstone exploring the Falls — the caption reads "Exploration: Mosi-oa-tunya — Victoria Falls". The words "Mosi-oa-tunya" meaning "The smoke that thunders".

It comes as no surprise that the first postage stamp issued connected with Dr Livingstone should feature the Victoria Falls. Rhodesia or the British South Africa Company as it was known then, issued stamps in 1905 to mark the visit of the British Association and the opening of the Victoria Falls Bridge.

It was Cecil Rhodes who ordered a survey to be carried out for a railway bridge to be built as close as possible to the Falls so that "Passengers would feel the spray" as they crossed. The bridge 364 feet above the Zambesi was built by the Cleveland Bridge Company of Darlington, England and officially opened by Professor Darwin, President of the British Association fifty years after Dr Livingstone first saw the Falls. Throughout the entire construction of the bridge only two people lost their lives. Another bridge called Knife Edge also at the Victoria Falls was featured on a definitive stamp from Zambia in 1975.

Right: The Victoria Falls, discovered in 1855 and named by Livingstone after Queen Victoria.

25

Postmark and stamps from Southern Rhodesia and Zambia featuring the Victoria Falls.

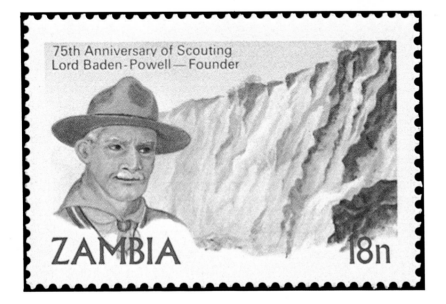

In 1931 the Falls were again featured, this time on stamps of Southern Rhodesia with a similar view to the British South Africa Company issue of 1905 and these stamps again appeared in Southern Rhodesia during May, 1932 but with a slight alteration in the border and the wording "British South Africa Company" changed to read "Southern Rhodesia".

To mark the Silver Jubilee of King George V in 1935, four stamps in common design were issued showing the Victoria Falls with African animals superimposed in the foreground. The Coronation of King George VI was also commemorated in Southern Rhodesia by four stamps in common design showing the Victoria Falls and railway bridge with a train crossing. In 1940 Southern Rhodesia marked the golden jubilee of the British South Africa Company by showing an excellent view of the Victoria Falls bridge on a stamp, and in 1953 a definitive stamp showed a view of the Falls and this was the last stamp issued by Southern Rhodesia to feature the famous Falls.

During 1953 Northern Rhodesia marked the centenary of the birth of Cecil Rhodes by issuing stamps showing in the background of the design the Victoria Falls and railway bridge.

Rhodesia and Nyasaland issued two stamps on 15th June, 1955 to mark the centenary of the discovery of the Victoria Falls by showing for the first time on any stamp a portrait of the famous explorer with the Falls in the background. The second stamp showed crossing the Falls 1855 style and by aeroplane 1955 style.

Right:
Rhodesia and
Nyasaland
stamp showing
the Eastern
Cataract and
Zambian
stamp
featuring
President
Kaunda at
the falls.

Previous to this, Dr Livingstone had yet to appear on a postage stamp, although his friend H. M. Stanley was commemorated on stamps issued by the Belgian Congo in 1928 to mark the 50th anniversary of his exploration of the Congo.

The first Rhodesia and Nyasaland definitive released in 1959 shows on one of the values the eastern cataract of the Falls and the Rhodesian decimal definitives issued in 1970 shows on one of the values the Victoria Falls under the heading of "Tourism". The following year this stamp was reprinted, the only alteration being in the value of the stamp. The view on these two stamps show the Devils Cataract, an awesome sight with a drop of some 200 feet. Rhodesia's 1978 definitives again feature the Falls on their top value stamp of two dollars and again under the banner of Zimbabwe in 1980.

Zambia, formerly Northern Rhodesia shows President Kenneth David Kaunda with the Falls in the background

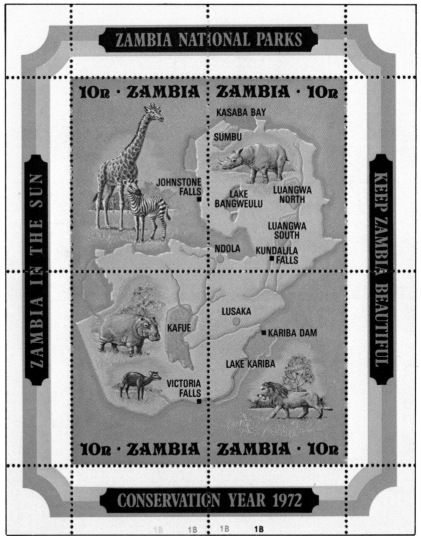

Zambian 1972 Conservation Year souvenir sheet based on the National Parks which includes the Victoria Falls.

*Top left:
Dr Livingstone on a Rhodesian stamp.
Above: Southern Rhodesian stamp showing the Victoria Falls Bridge.
Left: Northern Rhodesian stamp featuring the Victoria Falls and Railway Bridge.*

Left: An impressive view of the Victoria Falls on a high value stamp from Zimbabwe.

on a stamp issued to mark the Independence of Zambia in 1964.

It is interesting to note here that President Kaunda's father, the late David Kaunda was himself a missionary pioneer, and congregations formed as a result of his work have now become part of the United Church of Zambia. Both President Kaunda and his father had strong connections with Church of Scotland Missions. Finally, Conservation Year 1972 saw the Zambian Post Office issue stamps and a souvenir sheet, based on the Zambian National Parks featuring a map which included the Victoria Falls and in 1983 to commemorate the 75th anniversary of scouting showing Lord Baden Powell and the Falls.

Statistics: Height 355 feet, Width 1¼ miles. Water flow over the Falls — annual average 47 million gallons per minute. The Falls are twice as high and one and a half times as wide as the Niagara Falls.

Above: Sir Roderick Murchison (in white) and Dr Livingstone (circled) at a Royal Geographical Society picnic party.

Above: Stamp from Kenya, Uganda and Tanganyika featuring the Murchison Falls.

AFTER waiting a number of weeks at Quilimane, Dr Livingstone boarded a British gun-boat for Mauritius, and eventually after narrowly being shipwrecked in the Mediterranean he reached England on 9th December, 1856.

Dr Livingstone by now was a national hero and honours were poured upon him. The highlight at this time being a visit to Windsor Castle to meet Queen Victoria. As a gold medallist of the Royal Geographical Society he addressed members in London and met his life-long friend, Sir Roderick Murchison, a Scot like himself who was President of the Society. On hearing of Sir Roderick's death Livingstone wrote at Unyayembe on 3rd July, 1872 — "The best friend I ever had — warm, true, abiding — he loved me more than I deserved. He looks down on me still".

Like Dr Livingstone, Sir Roderick has also been featured on African postage stamps and indirectly Dr Livingstone was responsible, for it was the Doctor who

COMMEMORANT L'EXPLORATION DE L'AFRIQUE PAR STANLEY ET LIVINGSTONE

POSTE AERIENNE

15 F

REPUBLIQUE DU BURUNDI

Left: Stamp from Burundi showing Dr Livingstone writing his diaries in an African hut.

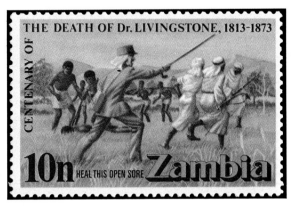

Right: Stamp from Zambia showing Dr Livingstone chasing the slave traders with the wording "Heal This Open Sore".

THE DEATH OF Dr. LIVINGSTONE, 1813-1873

CENTENARY OF

10n HEAL THIS OPEN SORE Zambia

named the Falls on the Zambesi after Murchison. The Murchison Falls and a hippo were featured on a stamp from Kenya, Uganda and Tanganyika in 1960, while Uganda also show the same Falls on a stamp issued in 1962. An East African tourist issue of 1966 also honours Murchison by featuring the Falls.

During his stay in Britain he began his first book under the title "Missionary Travels" which was destined to win a world-wide reputation as a single and complete volume of his travels in that strange land. Livingstone of course wrote a great deal during his long stay in Africa by way of correspondence to friends and his own diaries and a stamp issued by Burundi in 1973 shows Dr Livingstone sitting in an African hut writing his diaries.

Dr Livingstone was in great demand wherever he went, Oxford, Cambridge and Glasgow Universities granted him honorary degrees and he received the freedom of London, Edinburgh, Dundee, Hamilton, Glasgow and

Newstead (Notts). A special airmail letter issued by the British Post Office in 1975 to mark the 800th anniversary of the founding of Glasgow, shows an outline of the Livingstone statue which is situated close to Glasgow Cathedral.

Dr Livingstone used every opportunity while at home to publicise the horrors of the slave trade in Africa which was carried on by the Arabs with the support of the Portuguese. A stamp which aptly shows Dr Livingstone's concern for these unfortunate people was issued by Zambia in 1973 to mark the centenary of his death and shows the explorer chasing the slave traders away with the caption "Heal this open sore".

On 8th February, 1858 he was appointed British Consul for East Africa and the districts of the interior, and at the same time was offered the leadership of a new expedition which became known as the "Zambesi Expedition".

Right: Village scene on Lake Nyasa.

1858
1860

RETURN TO AFRICA

RETURN TO AFRICA

On 8th March, 1858 Dr Livingstone, his family and members of the Zambesi Expedition left England on board the steamer "Pearl" sailing via the Cape of Good Hope and arrived at the mouth of the Zambesi during the month of May. Among the members of the Expedition was Livingstone's brother Charles, who had recently returned from America and artist Thomas Baines, who was to become the most prolific South African painter of the nineteenth century. Unfortunately, owing to a dispute, reputedly with Charles Livingstone, Baines was dismissed from the Expedition within a year on a charge of mis-appropriating the stores of the Expedition. Baines was born in England in 1820 and died in 1875.

Thomas Baines was the subject of a single stamp from Rhodesia in 1975 and four stamps from South Africa later the same year and the paintings featured on these four stamps give an excellent impression of what Southern Africa looked like during the Livingstone era. A few days after arriving at the mouth of the Zambesi the party proceeded up the river in the "Ma Robert". This small steam launch built by Laird Brothers, Birkenhead weighed 23 tons and was named after the explorer's wife. The launch had been brought from

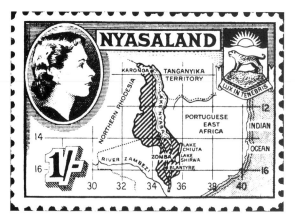

Above: Thomas Baines commemorated on a stamp from Rhodesia.

Left: Map stamp from Nyasaland showing Blantyre and Lakes Nyasa (Malawi) and Shirwa.

Four paintings of South Africa by Thomas Baines who was a member of Livingstone's Zambesi Expedition.
The stamps were issued in 1975 by the Republic of South Africa.

33

Above and left: Stamps from Malawi and Nyasaland featuring scenes on Lake Malawi.

Britain packed in sections for use on the river. During November of that year they came across the impassable barrier of the Kebrabasa Rapids and during January and April of 1859 explored the Shire River and discovered Lake Shirwa on 18th April. Lake Nyasa or Lake Malawi as it is now known was discovered on 2nd September, 1859.

A stamp issued by Nyasaland in 1954 features a map of this area and show Lakes Nyasa and Shirwa. Two other stamps issued at the same time show a boatman on Lake Nyasa and a native fishing village beside the Lake.

Nyasaland became Malawi in 1964 with Dr Hastings Banda as Prime Minister, he was later to become the first President, and it is also interesting to note that like President Kaunda of Zambia he also had connections with a Church of Scotland Mission where he received part of his education.

Lake Nyasa, renamed Lake Malawi has also been featured on a number of stamps from Malawi one issue of note being in 1967 which was devoted to steamers connected with the Lake.

Before returning from the first Zambesi Expedition Dr Livingstone made a second visit to the Victoria Falls on 9th August, 1860 before arriving at Tete on 23rd November. A definitive stamp issued by Zambia in 1975 shows the source of the Zambesi River together with Zambia's Independence Monument.

Livingstone's steam-launch, the 'Ma-Robert' on the Zambesi.

IN response to Dr Livingstone's many letters to England about the advantage of opening up the Shire Valley and the shores of Lake Nyasa for the purpose of founding a Colony, members of the Universities Mission to Central Africa with Bishop Mackenzie at their head, arrived off the Zambesi on 31st January, 1861. The steamer "Pioneer" also arrived at the same time, having been sent by the government on Dr Livingstone's request. The "Ma Robert" had succumbed making her final exit on a sandbank near Sena.

Dr Livingstone and his party with the aid of the "Pioneer" spent most of 1861 exploring the Rovuma River and Lake Nyasa, Magomero in Southern Nyasaland being established as the main base.

On 31st January, 1862 the "Lady Nyasa" was delivered in sections by HMS "Gorgon" at the mouth of the Zambesi. The "Lady Nyasa" had been ordered through Dr Livingstone's friend James Young, "Sir Paraffin" and was built by Messrs Tod and McGregor at Meadowside, Partick on the River Clyde, Scotland.

'Ma-Robert', Mrs Livingstone daughter of Dr Robert Moffat.

Rhodesian stamp
featuring the
Baobab Tree.

Mrs Livingstone's grave at Shupanga.

Mrs Livingstone was also on board the "Gorgon", she had been in England since parting from her husband at Capetown. Unfortunately, she was to die three months later on 27th April, 1862 at Shupanga, and was buried the following day under the shadow of a giant Baobab tree. Sailors from the "Gorgon" mounted guard for several nights over her grave.

The Baobab tree has been featured on a number of stamps, the most interesting being issued by Rhodesia in 1967 for Nature Conservation Week, and Botswana in 1968, issued a stamp showing a painting of Baobab trees by Thomas Baines.

AFTER the launching of the "Lady Nyasa" on 23rd June, 1862 further exploration took place on the Rovuma River, a return to the Zambesi and a further journey to Lake Nyasa with the intention of launching the "Lady Nyasa" there. However, this was not to be, and on 2nd July, 1863 Dr Livingstone received a despatch from Earl Russell in London recalling the Expedition.

Kongone — Livingstone's station on the Zambesi Delta.

The Clydesdale Bank 'Livingstone' ten pound note first issued in 1972. An encapsulated note presented by the Bank can be seen in the Kamuzu Academy, Malawi.

A native craft on a stamp from Zanzibar.

DISAPPOINTED by the alleged failure of the Zambesi Expedition Dr Livingstone decided that before he could penetrate Africa again, he would require to raise more funds. This could be done by selling the "Lady Nyasa" or returning to England and raise money there. He resolved to try the first.

The Portuguese offered to buy the ship, but Dr Livingstone refused to sell on the grounds that it could be used in the slave trade. He sailed up the coast to Zanzibar but the offers he received there were absurdly small, he decided therefore to cross the Indian Ocean and try his luck in Bombay and on the last day of April, 1864 started on his perilous journey to India in the "Lady Nyasa".

Never in Livingstone's wildest dreams could he have imagined that some 117 years later the Clydesdale Bank Limited would issue a ten pound note which featured the famous explorer and a scene from Africa.

A native craft pictured on a stamp issued in Zanzibar in 1913 would have been a familiar sight to Dr Livingstone while the same country issued a stamp in 1957 showing a map of the East African Coast which would also have been familiar.

After a brief stay in India where he also visited Poona, Surat and Nazik he left the "Lady Nyasa" in Bombay still unsold and sailed for England where he arrived on 23rd July, 1864.

During his stay in England he continued his writings, visited his many friends, including a stay with the Duke of Argyll in Inveraray, Scotland and from there went to Ulva, the home of his ancestors. In the spring of 1865 he sailed again for Africa via Bombay in India.

Dr Livingstone's eldest son Robert who was born in Africa in 1845 was to die in the United States of America in 1864 of wounds he received while fighting for the North somewhere near Richmond. He had enlisted under the name of "Rupert Vincent" as a private in the Third New Hampshire Regiment and is believed to have been buried in the US National Cemetery, Gettysburg, Pennsylvania.

Livingstone's house, Zanzibar.

WHEN Dr Livingstone arrived in Bombay he succeeded in finding a purchaser for the "Lady Nyasa", but unfortunately the most he was offered was £2,300 — the vessel had cost nearly £6,000. He decided to sell, and lodged the cash in an Indian Bank, which subsequently failed.

Dr Livingstone left Bombay and arrived at Zanzibar on 28th January, 1866 and after a slight delay left by a British gunboat for the African mainland.

When Dr Livingstone again set off for the interior among his party were Susi and Chuma, his faithful servants. The Doctor also had with him three tame Indian buffaloes, six camels some mules and donkeys on

Susi and Chuma, the faithful servants who missed Livingstone's funeral in Westminster Abbey owing to a misunderstanding.

Rhodesia and Nyasaland stamp issued in 1959 featuring Lake Bangweulu.

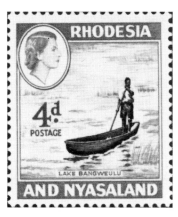

Kenya-Uganda-Tanganyika stamp issued in 1958 featuring Lake Tanganyika.

which he hoped to carry out tests on their reaction to the tse-tse fly, this experiment turned out to be unsuccessful.

The buffaloes and camel can be seen on a stamp issued by India in 1954. On 8th August, 1866 the party reached Lake Nyasa and crossed the Luangwa Valley and reached Lake Tanganyika — the south end of the Lake being reached on 2nd April, 1867. Two map stamps of East Africa showing Lake Tanganyika were issued by Kenya, Uganda and Tanganyika to mark the centenary of the discovery of Lakes Tanganyika and Victoria by Burton and Speke in 1858.

Dr Livingstone was to discover two further lakes on 8th November, 1867 Lake Mweru and on 18th July, 1868 Lake Bangweulu. The latter was featured on a stamp from Rhodesia and Nyasaland in 1959, and a stamp from Zambia in 1972.

During these years Dr Livingstone suffered many illnesses, the constant soakings and continual wading of rivers and swamps coupled with the absence of medicinal remedies were beginning to take their toll.

The party reached Ujiji on the eastern shore of Lake Tanganyika for the second time on 5th November, 1871, although the date of arrival according to Dr Livingstone was 23rd October, it is thought however that he was thirteen days out. It was here some days later that the famous meeting took place between Dr Livingstone and Henry M. Stanley the Welsh-born American journalist explorer.

FAMOUS MEETING WITH STANLEY

HENRY Morton Stanley, a journalist sent by his newspaper *The New York Herald* to find the great explorer, first met him at Ujiji in the heart of Africa on 10th November, 1871. On meeting Dr Livingstone, Stanley is believed to have said "Dr Livingstone, I presume?" and these words have since become famous, and often quoted.

Stanley's account of the meeting is as follows:

"We arrived at the summit, travel across and arrive at its western rim, and — pause reader — the port of Ujiji is below us embowered in the palms, only five hundred yards from us. At this grand moment we do not think of the hundreds of miles we have marched, of the hundreds of hills that we have ascended and descended, of the many forests we have traversed, of the jungles and thickets that annoyed us, the fervid salt plains that blistered our feet, of the hot suns that scorched us, nor the dangers and difficulties . . . A volley from fifty guns roars like a salute from the battery of artillery . . . Before we had gone a hundred yards our repeated volleys had the effect desired. We had awaken Ujiji to the knowledge that a caravan was coming, and the people were witnessed rushing up in hundreds to meet us. The mere sight of the flags informed everyone immediately that we were a caravan. . . . We were now about three hundred yards from the village of Ujiji and the crowds

REPUBLIQUE DU BURUNDI

Stamp from Burundi featuring the now famous meeting.

are dense about me. Suddenly I heard a voice on my right say, 'Good morning, sir!'

"Startled at hearing this greeting in the midst of such a crowd of black people, I turn sharply around in search of the man, and see him at my side, with the blackest of faces, but animated and joyous — a man dressed in a long white shirt, with a turban of American sheeting around his woolly head, and I ask: 'Who the mischief are you?' 'I am Susi, the servant of Dr Livingstone', said he, smiling, and showing a gleaming row of teeth.

'What! Is Dr Livingstone here?'

'. . . Now, you Susi, run, and tell the Doctor I am coming' . . . What would I not have given for a bit of friendly wilderness, where, unseen, I might vent my joy in some mad freak . . . but I must not let my face betray my emotions . . . So I did that which I thought most dignified. I pushed back the crowds, and, passing from the rear, walked down a living avenue of people, until I came in front of the semi-circle of Arabs, in front of which stood the white man with the grey beard. As I advanced slowly towards him I noticed he was pale,

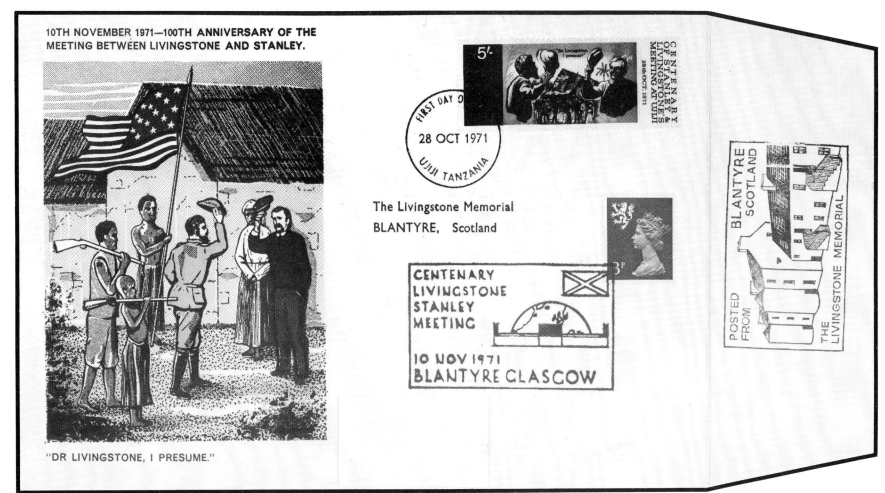

Souvenir envelope commemorating the 100th Anniversary of the meeting between Livingstone and Stanley, bearing the Ujiji and Blantyre (Scotland) postmarks.

looked wearied, had a grey beard, wore a bluish cap with a faded gold band round it, had on a red sleeved waistcoat, and a pair of grey tweed trousers.

I would have run to him, only I was a coward in the presence of such a mob — would have embraced him, only he being an Englishman, I did not know how he would receive me; so I did what cowardice and false pride suggested was the best thing — walked deliberately to him, took off my hat, and said: 'Dr Livingstone, I presume'.

'Yes', said he, with a kind of smile, lifting his cap slightly. I replaced my hat on my head, and he put on his cap, and we both grasp hands, and I then say aloud: 'I thank God, Doctor, I have been permitted to see you'. He answered, 'I feel thankful that I am here to welcome you'. "

This famous meeting has been featured on many postage stamps and allied material. One of the most interesting from a philatelic point of view was a special commemorative envelope and postmark which was sponsored by the David Livingstone Trust in 1971. The envelope illustrates in colour the famous meeting and bears two stamps and cancellations which are unique.

The first stamp of five shillings value was issued in East Africa to mark the centenary of the meeting at Ujiji and shows Dr Livingstone and Stanley, the stamp was cancelled at Ujiji, Tanzania on 28th October, 1971. The second stamp on the envelope a threepence Scottish regional definitive was cancelled at Blantyre, Scotland a

Henry M. Stanley

few days later on 10th November, 1971. The special postmark features part of a memorial called the "World Fountain" which was created by sculptor C. d'O Pilkington Jackson and can be seen today at the David Livingstone National Memorial at Blantyre.

Only 175 of these envelopes were serviced at Ujiji and Blantyre and carry the signature of Mr William Cunningham, the warden at Blantyre as being authentic. Other countries which have issued stamps featuring this now famous meeting include Botswana, Zambia and Burundi.

Dr Livingstone and Stanley were together for about four months during which time they became great friends and went on a number of explorations which included a visit to the north end of Lake Tanganyika and on 27th December, 1871 they set out for Unyanyembe where he parted with Stanley on 14th March, 1872. Stanley had been unsuccessful in persuading Dr Livingstone to return with him. On parting Dr Livingstone gave Stanley his famous "Red Shirt" and this can be seen today together with a vast collection of relics etc. at the National Memorial at Blantyre.

A stamp issued by Botswana in 1973 shows Dr Livingstone and Stanley together in a boat during one of their excursions.

Top left: Stamps issued by the British Post Office in 1973 under the title of British Explorers. Below left: Stamp from Burundi commemorating the Centenary of African Exploration and stamps from Zambia and Botswana marking the centenary of the death of Dr Livingstone.

Livingstone's last day's march.

DEATH AT CHITAMBO'S VILLAGE

AFTER the parting with Stanley, Dr Livingstone left Unyanyembe for Lake Tanganyika on 25th August, 1872. He journeyed down the east side of the Lake and by January, 1873 had arrived at Lake Bangweula this time from the north east side.

When Dr Livingstone arrived at Ilala, sick and weary, his devoted servants built a hut in Chitambo's village to shelter him in what was to be his last illness. He lived only four days in the hut dying on 1st May, 1873. He was found by his two faithful servants Susi and Chuma kneeling by his bed, his face resting on his hands and had died while in the act of praying to God.

Dr Livingstone had died while in the act of praying to God.

Early postcard featuring Livingstone's Hut, Wemyss Bay, Scotland. The hut was built by Chuma and Susi in the grounds of James Young (Mr Paraffin) of Kelly a close friend and supporter of Livingstone.

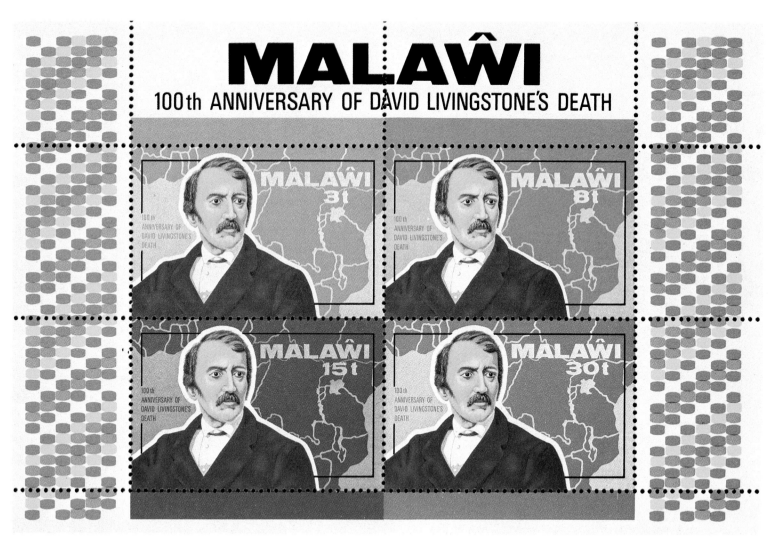

Souvenir sheet issued by Malawi in 1973 to mark the 100th Anniversary of the death of Dr Livingstone.

Right: Envelope and invitation to the funeral of Dr Livingstone in Westminster Abbey, London, 1874.

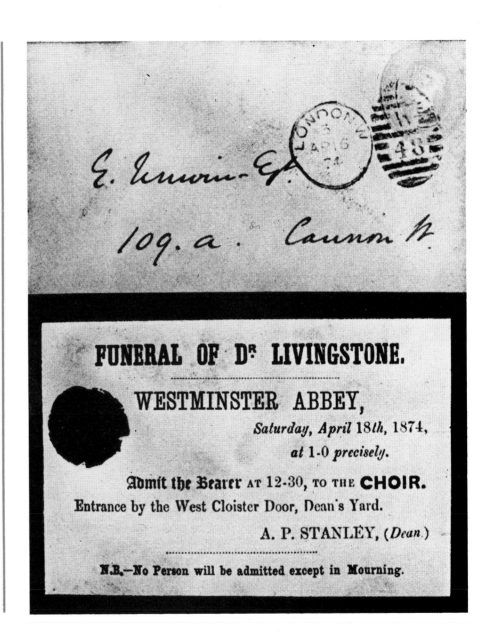

Malawi issued a stamp in 1967 featuring the steamer "Ilala I" and a further stamp showing "Ilala II" in 1975 both ships were called "Ilala" after the district where Dr Livingstone had died.

In 1973 a number of countries issued stamps to mark the centenary of the death of Dr Livingstone and one of the stamps in a set of six from Zambia shows the tree at Chitambo under which the heart of Dr Livingstone was buried.

The remainder of Dr Livingstone's body was embalmed and his followers which included Susi, Chuma and Jacob Wainwright carried his body and belongings 1500 miles to the coast, arriving at Bagamoyo during February of 1874. The body was then shipped to England and was buried in Westminster Abbey on 18th April, 1874 with national honours.

Among the mourners were Dr Robert Moffat his father-in-law, Henry Stanley and Livingstone's African servant Jacob Wainwright. His two faithful servants Susi and Chuma unfortunately arrived too late for the funeral, owing to a mis-understanding.

Among the many wreaths was one from Queen Victoria. The inscription on the coffin read:

"David Livingstone
born at Blantyre, Lanarkshire, Scotland
19th March, 1813
Died at Ilala, Central Africa,
4th May, 1873"

Above left: Stamp from Zambia featuring the tree at Chitambo under which the heart of Dr Livingstone was buried.
Above right: Stamp from Malawi featuring "Ilala 1" on Lake Malawi.

Above: Livingstone's embalmed body being carried the 1500 miles to the coast.

"IN ZAMBIA HIS HEART WAS BURIED AND RESTS......"

BROUGHT BY FAITHFUL HANDS
OVER LAND AND SEA
HERE RESTS
DAVID LIVINGSTONE,
MISSIONARY,
TRAVELLER,
PHILANTHROPIST,
BORN MARCH 19.1813.
AT BLANTYRE. LANARKSHIRE.
DIED MAY 1.1873,
AT CHITAMBOS VILLAGE, ULALA.

FOR 30 YEARS HIS LIFE WAS SPENT
IN AN UNWEARIED EFFORT
TO EVANGELIZE THE NATIVE RACES,
TO EXPLORE THE UNDISCOVERED SECRETS,
TO ABOLISH THE DESOLATING SLAVE TRADE,
OF CENTRAL AFRICA,
WHERE WITH HIS LAST WORDS HE WROTE,
"ALL I CAN ADD IN MY SOLITUDE, IS,
MAY HEAVEN'S RICH BLESSING COME DOWN
ON EVERY ONE. AMERICAN, ENGLISH, OR TURK,
WHO WILL HELP TO HEAL
THIS OPEN SORE OF THE WORLD."

REPUBLIC OF ZAMBIA
OFFICIAL FIRST DAY COVER
1ST MAY 1973

Above: The wording on the brass plaque which marks the burial place of Dr Livingstone in Westminster Abbey.

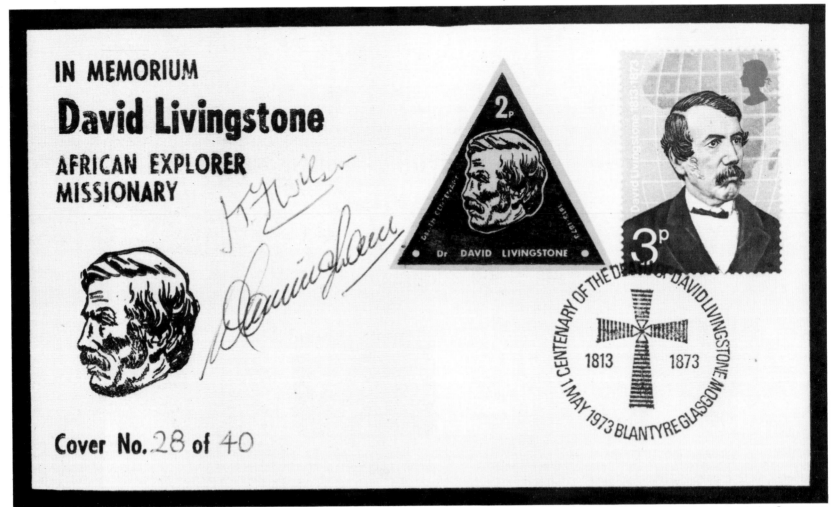

IN MEMORIUM

David Livingstone

AFRICAN EXPLORER
MISSIONARY

2p

Dr DAVID LIVINGSTONE

3p

CENTENARY OF THE DEATH OF DAVID LIVINGSTONE. GLASGOW
1813 1873
1 MAY 1973 BLANTYRE GLASGOW

Cover No. 28 of 40

One of forty Special Commemorative envelopes to mark the Centenary of the death of David Livingstone autographed by W. Cunningham, the warden at Blantyre and Dr Hubert Wilson, grandson of Dr Livingstone.